The Ultimate Netball Trivia Book

KATIE SMITH

THE UTIMATE NETBALL TRIVIA BOOK

Copyright © 2023 Katie Smith

All rights reserved.

ISBN: 9798857144930

For all those that love netball,
this book is for you

Table of Contents

HUMBLE BEGINNINGS 4
WORLD NETBALL 14
PLAY BY THE RULES 20
THE NETBALL WORLD CUP 34
INTERNATIONAL ICONS 40
ANZ PREMIERSHIP 52
SUNCORP SUPER NETBALL 58
ENGLISH SUPER LEAGUE 64
QUAD SERIES 72
CONSTELLATION CUP 76
TRANS-TASMAN NETBALL LEAGUE 82
COMMONWEALTH BANK TROPHY 92
NATIONAL BANK CUP 98
THE BUSINESS OF NETBALL 102

THE UTIMATE NETBALL TRIVIA BOOK

Every effort was made to ensure all information was accurate at the time of publishing.

HUMBLE BEGINNINGS

Question 1.
Q: What sport did Netball originate from?
A: Basketball

Question 2.
Q: What name was Netball originally given?
A: Women's Basketball

Question 3.
Q: What country did the first game of Netball occur in?
A: England

Question 4.
Q: How did Netball spread around the world?
A: Through schools, specifically Physical Education teachers, in the British Empire.

THE UTIMATE NETBALL TRIVIA BOOK

Question 5.
Q: When was the first official set of rules codified for Netball?
A: 1900 for the Physical Education Association

Question 6.
Q: What institution was the first game of Netball played at?
A: Bergman Österberg physical training college in Dartford, England

Question 7.
Q: What was the name of the woman credited with founding Netball?
A: Martina Bergman-Österberg

Question 8.
Q: What was the institution that published the first set of Netball rules?
A: The Ling Association

Question 9.
Q: When did the first international game of Netball occur?
A: 1938

Question 10.
Q: What countries played in the first international game of Netball?
A: Australia vs. New Zealand

THE UTIMATE NETBALL TRIVIA BOOK

Question 11.

Q: Why were the rules of Netball modified from Basketball?

A: Changes in rules are often attributed to Victorian women's attire in the period such as long skirts making dribbling the ball impractical and this is not inaccurate, other rule changes were more subtle and rooted in the belief that women's sport should not be overly competitive, rather should be played with a cooperative and "ladylike" spirit reflecting the accepted notion of femininity of the time. Rules such as the ball cannot be stolen ran with fall into this category.

Question 12.

Q: What major world events stopped International Netball Tests from occurring?

A: WWI, The Great Depression and WWII.

Question 13.

Q: What other movements was the creator of Netball associated with?

A: The Suffragette and Women's Emancipation Movements

Question 14.

Q: True or False – the creator of Netball was Swedish?

A: True

THE UTIMATE NETBALL TRIVIA BOOK

Question 15.
Q: What year did Netball arrive in Australia?
A: 1897 is the earliest there are reported matches of Netball in Australia

Question 16.
Q: What year did Netball arrive in New Zealand?
A: 1906

Question 17.
Q: Who bought Netball to New Zealand?
A: Reverand J.C. Jamieson

Question 18.
Q: In the New Zealand version of Netball, originally how many players were on the court at one time?
A: Nine

Question 19.
Q: How was Netball originally spread through the country of New Zealand?
A: Through schools.

Question 20.
Q: What equipment was used for the first games of Netball?
A: Grass courts and baskets tied to posts.

THE UTIMATE NETBALL TRIVIA BOOK

Question 21.
Q: Which country developed the name Netball for the sport?
A: England

Question 22.
Q: When did Women's Basketball officially change its name to Netball everywhere in the world?
A: 1970

Question 23.
Q: What led to the changes in Women's Basketball that we see today in Netball about positions being only able to move in certain areas of the court?
A: When Clara Baer, a sports teacher in New Orleans, wrote to Naismith asking for a copy of the rules, the subsequent rules package contained a drawing of the court with lines penciled across it, simply to show the areas various players could best patrol. But Baer misinterpreted the lines and thought players couldn't leave those areas.

THE UTIMATE NETBALL TRIVIA BOOK

WORLD NETBALL

Question 24.
Q: What is the body that governs international netball?
A: World Netball

Question 25.
Q: What event was the catalyst for World Netball's creation?
A: A 1957 tour of the Australian Netball team of England and the need to codify rules for International Competitions.

Question 26.
Q: What city and country was the meeting to agreement on the creation of World Netball held in?
A: In Colombo, Sri Lanka, then known as Ceylon.

Question 27.
Q: What year was World Netball founded?
A: 1960

THE UTIMATE NETBALL TRIVIA BOOK

Question 28.
Q: Where is World Netball based?
A: Manchester, England

Question 29.
Q: What other names has World Netball had?
A: International Netball Federation, International Federation of Netball Associations.

Question 30.
Q: How many regions are there in World Netball (bonus points for being able to name them)?
A: Five – Africa, Asia, Americas, Europe and Oceania.

Question 31.
Q: How many countries are members of World Netball?
A: 65 Full Members and 23 Associate Members, 88 Members in Total

Question 32.
Q: How many founding countries of World Netball were there (bonus points for being able to name them all)?
A: Five – namely:
    Australia
    New Zealand
    England
    Wales
    South Africa

Question 33.
Q: What major Netball events does World Netball oversea?
A: The Netball World Cup, the Netball World Youth Cup and Fast5 Netball World Series.

Question 34.
Q: What year was Netball officially recognized as a sport by the International Olympic Committee?
A: 1995

Question 35.
Q: What are the other major functions of World Netball beyond organizing the World Netball Cup and other major tournaments?
A: They organize international rankings, are signatories to the Anti-Doping associations, and maintain the rules of the game for competition.

THE UTIMATE NETBALL TRIVIA BOOK

PLAY BY THE RULES

Question 36.
Q: How long is the court?
A: 30.5m

Question 37.
Q: How wide is the court?
A: 15.25m

Question 38.
Q: How tall is the hoop?
A: 3.05m

Question 39.
Q: How many players are on the court at one time?
A: 14 – 2 x teams of 7 each.

THE UTIMATE NETBALL TRIVIA BOOK

Question 40.
Q: How many players are allowed on a Netball team (include the bench players)?
A: 12

Question 41.
Q: How many seconds do you have to release the ball after it has been received?
A: 3 seconds.

Question 42.
Q: When is a point scored in Netball?
A: When a Goal Attack or Goal Shooter shoots the ball into the hoop.

Question 43.
Q: Name all seven positions in Netball?
A: Goal Shooter
    Goal Attack
    Wing Attack
    Center
    Wing Defense
    Goal Defense
    Goal Keeper

Question 44.
Q: A center player is offside when he or she enters which part of the court?
A: Goal Circle

THE UTIMATE NETBALL TRIVIA BOOK

Question 45.
Q: Why do Netball players have to wear bibs?
A: To identify the positions they play.

Question 46.
Q: How long is a Netball game?
A: 60 minutes.

Question 47.
Q: How many periods in a netball game?
A: Four quarters.

Question 48.
Q: How long is each quarter in Netball?
A: 15 minutes

Question 49.
Q: What is the name of the modified game of netball which includes goals worth multiple points, shortened games and rolling substitutions?
A: Fast5

Question 50.
Q: How long are quarters in a game of Fast5 Netball?
A: 6 minutes

Question 51.
Q: What colour do umpires wear?
A: White

THE UTIMATE NETBALL TRIVIA BOOK

Question 52.
Q: How many players in each team are allowed to enter the center third at one time?
A: Five – namely:
> Goal Attack
> Wing Attack
> Center
> Wing Defense
> Goal Defense

Question 53.
Q: What size ball are adult and professional Netball games played with?
A: Size 5

Question 54.
Q: How is the game restarted after a team scores a goal?
A: It is taken back to the center pass.

Question 55.
Q: A Netball court is divided into how many sections?
A: Three

Question 56.
Q: If a player moves with the ball beyond one step what is the infringement of the rules called?
A: Footwork (often called stepping)

THE UTIMATE NETBALL TRIVIA BOOK

Question 57.
Q: How far away from the player with the ball do you have to be to defend with your arms up?
A: 0.9m / 3 feet.

Question 58.
Q: What is the rules infringement called if a player puts their arms up within 0.9m of the player with the ball?
A: Obstruction

Question 59.
Q: What is the rules infringement called if a player knocks or runs into another player?
A: Contact

Question 60.
Q: Is on the line in or out?
A: In

Question 61.
Q: Are you allowed to bounce the ball?
A: Yes, but only once.

Question 62.
Q: Are you allowed to bat the ball?
A: Yes, but only once.

THE UTIMATE NETBALL TRIVIA BOOK

Question 63.
Q: Are you allowed to throw the ball to yourself?
A: No.

Question 64.
Q: Which player marks the Goal Shooter?
A: Goal Keeper

Question 65.
Q: Which player marks the Goal Attack?
A: Goal Defence

Question 66.
Q: Which player marks the Wing Attack?
A: Wing Defense

Question 67.
Q: Which player marks the Center?
A: Center

Question 68.
Q: Are you allowed to roll the ball in Netball?
A: No – you can do small bounces.

Question 69.
Q: What is the minimum distance that needs to between two players to pass the ball?
A: There is no official distance, there must be room for a third player to move between the passer and receiver.

THE UTIMATE NETBALL TRIVIA BOOK

Question 70.
Q: Can you play the ball off the post on a throw in and catch it yourself?
A: Yes, but both feet must have

Question 71.
Q: What is the diameter of the center circle?
A: 0.9m / 3 feet

THE UTIMATE NETBALL TRIVIA BOOK

THE NETBALL WORLD CUP

Question 72.
Q: Which three countries are the only to have won the Netball World Cup since the first competition?
A: Australia, New Zealand and Trinidad and Tobago.

Question 73.
Q: Which country has won the most titles at the Netball World Cup?
A: Australia – 12 wins.

Question 74.
Q: Where was the first Netball World Cup held?
A: Eastbourne, England

Question 75.
Q: What was the first Netball World Cup called?
A: World Netball Tournament

Question 76.
Q: How often are the World Championship held?
A: Every 4 years

Question 77.
Q: Which team was banned from the Netball World Championship for over 25 years?
A: South Africa

Question 78.
Q: Which team upset the Silver Ferns in the 1995 World Cup?
A: The South African Proteas

Question 79.
Q: What year was the World Cup first played on indoor courts?
A: 1991

Question 80.
Q: What year was the World Cup first broadcast live at primetime to markets in Australia and New Zealand on television?
A: 1991

THE UTIMATE NETBALL TRIVIA BOOK

Question 80.
Q: Who famously said after losing the World Cup Grand Final *"the winner tonight was netball"*?
A: Wai Taumaunu – Captain of the Silver Ferns in her post-game speech.

Question 81.
Q: Which country has hosted the world cup the most times?
A: Australia, New Zealand and England have all hosted the Netball World Cup three times each.

Question 82.
Q: What year was the first time a finals structure was added to the Netball World Cup instead of a round robin, first past the post type tournament?
A: 1991, when the tournament was hosted in Sydney.

Question 83.
Q: Who won the inaugural Netball World Championship?
A: Australia

INTERNATIONAL ICONS

Question 84.
Q: What is the name of the Australian National Netball Team?
A: Diamonds

Question 85.
Q: What is the name of the English National Netball Team?
A: Roses

Question 86.
Q: What is the name of the New Zealand National Netball Team?
A: Silver Ferns

Question 87.
Q: What is the name of the Jamacia National Netball Team?

A: The Sunshine Girls

Question 88.
Q: What is the name of the Scottish National Netball Team?
A: Thistles

Question 89.
Q: What is the name of the Welsh National Netball Team?
A: Feathers

Question 90.
Q: What is the name of the Barbados National Netball Team?
A: Bajan Gems

Question 91.
Q: What is the name of the Brunei National Netball Team?
A: Royal Bees

Question 92.
Q: What is the name of the Cook Islands National Netball Team?
A: Black Pearls

Question 93.
Q: What is the name of the Fiji National Netball Team?
A: Pearls

Question 94.
Q: What is the name of the Kenya National Netball Team?

A: Divas

Question 95.
Q: What is the name of the Malawi National Netball Team?
A: The Queens

Question 96.
Q: What is the name of the Namibia National Netball Team?
A: The Desert Jewels

Question 97.
Q: What is the name of the Papua New Guinean National Netball Team?
A: The Pepes

Question 98.
Q: What is the name of the Philippines National Netball Team?
A: Siklab Pilipinas

Question 99.
Q: What is the name of the Samoa National Netball Team?
A: Tifa Moana

Question 100.
Q: What is the name of the South African National Netball Team?
A: Proteas

Question 101.
Q: What is the name of the Sri Lankan National Netball Team?
A: Lionesses

Question 102.
Q: What is the name of the Tongan National Netball Team?
A: Tala

Question 103.
Q: What is the name of the Uganda National Netball Team?
A: She-Cranes

Question 104.
Q: What is the name of the Zimbabwe National Netball Team?
A: The Gems

Question 105.
Q: What is the name of the US National Netball Team?
A: The Flying Eagles

Question 106.
Q: What is the name of the Trinidad and Tobago National Netball Team?
A: The Calypso Girls

Question 107.

Q: Who is the most capped International Netballer of All-Time?

A: Irene Van Dyk – 217 caps

Question 108.

Q: What two countries has Irene Van Dyk played for?

A: South Africa & Silver Fern

Question 109.

Q: Name two players that have represented two different countries on the international stage?

A: 1. Irene Van Dyk
    2. Mo'onia Gerard
    3. Chelsea Pittman
    4. Leanna De Bruin
    5. Kadeen Corbin
    6. Sasha Corbin
    7. Catherine Tuivaiti

Question 110.

Q: Who is the most capped Australian Diamond of all time?

A: Liz Ellis

Question 111.

Q: How tall is Jhaniele Fowler-Reid?

A: 198cm

Question 112.
Q: What player is Netball Australia's highest honor for players annually for performance in domestic competitions and for the international award for Diamonds named after?
A: Liz Ellis – Australia's most capped international player ever.

Question 113.
Q: Which players is the only to have received the top Silver Ferns Netball award – Silver Ferns Player of the Year - twice?
A: Laura Langman

Question 114.
Q: Which New Zealand Silver Ferns coach is a Dame?
A: Noeline Taurua

Question 115.
Q: What English coach comes from a family of English sporting royalty?
A: Tracy Neville – her brother Phil Neville played professional football for Manchester United and currently assistant coaches the Canadian men's national soccer team.

Question 116.
Q: Which international player has played for three different countries?
A: Catherine Tuivaiti – Samoa, New Zealand and Tonga.

ANZ PREMIERSHIP

Question 117.
Q: What year did the ANZ Premiership start?
A: 2017 was the inaugural season.

Question 118.
Q: True or false – the Minor Premiers and the Grand Final winners were the same team 6 out of seven seasons the competition has been running?
A: True

Question 119.
Q: Which club has the most Premierships wins?
A: Central Pulse, winning 3 titles.

Question 120.
Q: Who is the most successful coach in the ANZ Premiership, winning three premierships?
A: Yvette McCausland-Durie

Question 121.
Q: How many teams compete in the ANZ Premiership (bonus points for being able to name them)?
A: Six, namely –
    Central Pulse
    Mainland Tactix
    Northern Mystics
    Southern Steel
    Waikato Bay of Plenty Magic
    Northern Stars

Question 122.
Q: Which player has been the league's leading scorer three times?
A: Grace Nweke – 2020, 2021 and 2023.

Question 123.
Q: Who is the only player to win ANZ Premiership player of the year twice?
A: Jane Watson

Question 124.
Q: Who is the broadcast partner of the ANZ Premiership?
A: Sky Sports

Question 125.
Q: What was the new franchise introduced when the ANZ Premiership began that had not competed in the predecessor Trans-Tasman Netball League tournament?
A: Northern Stars

Question 126.
Q: Which team went undefeated in the inaugural season of the ANZ Premiership?
A: Southern Steel

Question 127.
Q: Which team has appeared in four successive grand finals?
A: Central Pulse

Question 128.
Q: Which three franchises are the only to have won the regular season minor premiership?
A: Central Pulse, Southern Steel and Northern Mystics

Question 129.
Q: Who is the naming rights sponsor of the league?
A: ANZ Bank

SUNCORP SUPER NETBALL

Question 130.
Q: What year did Suncorp Super Netball commence?
A: 2017

Question 131.
Q: How many teams compete in Suncorp Super Netball Season (bonus points for being able to name them all)?
A: Eight, namely –
    Adelaide Thunderbirds
    Collingwood Magpies
    Giants
    Melbourne Vixens
    New South Wales Swifts
    Queensland Firebirds
    Sunshine Coast Lightning
    West Coast Fever

THE UTIMATE NETBALL TRIVIA BOOK

Question 132.
Q: Who is the streaming partner of Suncorp Super Netball?
A: Kayo

Question 133.
Q: Who is the broadcasting partner of Suncorp Super Netball?
A: Fox Sports

Question 134.
Q: What company is the naming sponsor of the league?
A: Suncorp Group

Question 135.
Q: What were the three expansion teams added that had not competed in the predecessor tournament the Trans-Tasman tournament?
A: Giants, Lightning and Collingwood Magpies.

Question 136.
Q: Which two teams are the most successful in the history of the league?
A: New South Wales Swifts and Sunshine Coast Lightning with two titles each.

Question 137.
Q: Who has won the player of the year award 5 out of 6 times it has bene awarded?
A: Jhaniele Fowler-Reid

Question 138.

Q: Players from five different nationalities have been awarded the Suncorp Super Netball Grand Final MVP award. What are these five countries?

A: South Africa – Karla Mostert
     Australia – Caitlin Basset, Maddy Turner and Sasha Glasgow
     England – Eleanor Cardwell
     Malawi – Mwai Kumwenda
     Trinidad and Tobago – Samantha Wallace

Question 139.

Q: Which player has won the scoring title five times?
A: Jhaniele Fowler-Reid

ENGLISH SUPER LEAGUE

Question 140.
Q: Which is the only country that is part of the United Kingdon to not feature a team in the English Super League?
A: Northern Ireland

Question 141.
Q: How many teams compete in the English Super League (bonus points for being able to name them all)?
A: Ten, namely –
    Celtic Dragons
    London Pulse
    Loughborough Lightning
    Manchester Thunder
    Saracens Mavericks
    Severn Stars
    Strathclyde Sirens
    Surrey Storm

Team Bath

Question 142.
Q: There are four defunct teams, can you name them all?
A: Glasgow Wildcats
     Leeds Carnegie
     Team Northumbria
     Wasps Netball

Question 143.
Q: What year did the Super Netball League commence?
A: 2005 - 2006

Question 144.
Q: Who is the broadcast partner of the Netball Super League?
A: Sky Sports

Question 145.
Q: Who is the most successful team in the history of the league?
A: Team Bath – winning 5 titles.

THE UTIMATE NETBALL TRIVIA BOOK

THE UTIMATE NETBALL TRIVIA BOOK

Question 146.

Q: How many teams existed in the founding inaugural season?

A: Eight, namely –
- Brunel Hurricanes
- Celtic Dragons
- Galleria Mavericks
- Leeds Carnegie
- Loughborough Lightning
- Northern Thunder
- Team Bath
- Team Northumbria

Question 147.

Q: How many teams have won at least one title?

A: Six, namely 0
- Team Bath – 2005/2006, 2006/2007, 2008/2009, 2009/2010 & 2013.
- Manchester Thunder – 2012, 2014, 2019 & 2022
- Mavericks – 2007/2008, 2011
- Surrey Storm – 2017 & 2018
- Loughborough Lightning – 2021 & 2023

Question 148.

Q: What company holds the naming rights sponsorship to the league?

A: VitalityHealth

Question 149.
Q: Which player has won Netball Superleague player of the season three times?
A: Pamela Cookey

QUAD SERIES

Question 150.
Q: Which four countries compete in the Quad Series?
A: Australia, New Zealand, England and South Africa

Question 151.
Q: How often does the Quad Series occur?
A: Annually

Question 152.
Q: What Rugby tournament is the series modelled off?
A: Six Nations

Question 153.
Q: What is the governing body of the partnerships between the national bodies that overseas the series?
A: SANZEA

THE UTIMATE NETBALL TRIVIA BOOK

Question 154.
Q: What was the year of the inaugural tournament?
A: 2016

Question 155.
Q: Which country has won the tournament the most times and how many times?
A: Australia – 7 titles.

Question 156.
Q: When did discussions about the Quad series begin?
A: 2012 – 4 years before the first games were held.

Question 157.
Q: What was the original name of the series?
A: International Netball Super Series.

Question 158.
Q: Who are the four broadcast partners for the series across the four nations that compete currently?
A: Australia – Fox Sports
UK – Sky Sports
New Zealand – Sky Sports
South Africa - SuperSport

Question 159.
Q: What is the format of the tournament?
A: A round robin followed by two games – a final and a third-place final.

CONSTELLATION CUP

Question 160.
Q: Which two countries play in the Constellation Cup?
A: Australia and New Zealand

Question 161.
Q: What year was the inaugural Constellation Cup played?
A: 2010

Question 162.
Q: How many tests are there in the Constellation Cup Series?
A: It has been between 3 and 5 test matches, typically played over a week to ten days.

Question 163.
Q: What is the record for successive wins of the Constellation Cup and what country holds this?
A: Australia won 7 times between 2013 and 2019

Question 164.
Q: When did New Zealand first win the Constellation Cup?
A: 2012

Question 165.
Q: How many times has New Zealand won the Constellation Cup?
A: Twice – 2012 and 2021

Question 166.
Q: What tournament inspired the Constellation Cup?
A: The Bledisloe Cup – a Rugby Cup between New Zealand and Australia contested annually.

Question 167.
Q: What is the trophy for the Constellation Cup made of?
A: 3 Kilograms of Silver encrusted with 101 Diamonds (2.28 carats)

Question 168.
Q: How many times has the Constellation Cup been a sweep?
A: Twice – in 2017 and 2014 where Australia won 4-0.

Question 169.
Q: How is a draw decided in a four test match series?
A: An aggregation of the total points.

THE UTIMATE NETBALL TRIVIA BOOK

Question 170.

Q: Who are the current broadcast partners for the Constellation Cup (as of writing in 2023)?

A: Foxtel in Australia and Sky Sport in New Zealand

Question 171.

Q: What does the Constellation Cup symbolize?

A: The intensity of the rivalry between Australian and New Zealand netball as the best in the world.

TRANS-TASMAN NETBALL LEAGUE

Question 172.
Q: In what two countries were the teams that competed in the Trans-Tasman Netball League?
A: New Zealand & Australia

Question 173.
Q: What year did the Trans-Tasman Championship commence?
A: 2008

Question 174.
Q: How many years did the Trans-Tasman Championship run for?
A: 7 years – from 2008 to 2016

Question 175.
Q: Who won the inaugural Trans-Tasman Championship?
A: NSW Swifts

THE UTIMATE NETBALL TRIVIA BOOK

Question 176.
Q: Which team won the most championships?
A: Queensland Firebirds with 3 – 2011, 2015 & 2016

Question 177.
Q: How many teams were there in the Trans-Tasman Championship (bonus points for naming them all)?
A: Ten, namely –
    NSW Swifts
    QLD Firebirds
    Adelaide Thunderbirds
    Canterbury Tactix
    Central Pulse
    Melbourne Vixens
    Northern Mystics
    Southern Steele
    Waikato Bay of Plenty
    West Coast Fever

Question 178.
Q: Who was the only team to win back-to-back championships?
A: The Queensland Firebirds in 2015 & 2016

THE UTIMATE NETBALL TRIVIA BOOK

Question 179.
Q: Who was the most successful New Zealand team in the Trans-Tasman Championship?
A: Waikato Bay of Plenty Magic who were premiers in 2012 and were the only team in the competition's history, to contest the finals series every year.

Question 180.
Q: What were the two conferences that the competition was split into?
A: Australian and New Zealand

Question 181.
Q: True or False – in the first five seasons of the Trans-Tasman Netball League five different teams were champions?
A: True, namely –
    2008 – NSW Swifts
    2009 – Melbourne Vixens
    2010 – Adelaide Thunderbirds
    2011 – Queensland Firebirds
    2012 – Waikato Bay of Plenty Magic

Question 182.
Q: What is highest recorded attendance at a Trans-Tasman Netball League grand final?
A: Inaugural 2008 Final in Sydney at Acer Arena between the NSW Swifts and the Waikato Bay of Plenty Magic with 12,999 people attending the game.

Question 183.
Q: Who were the broadcast partners for the Trans-Tasman League?
A: Sky Sport in New Zealand and Fox Sport in Australia in 2008, 2013 – 2014, Network 10 2009 – 2012, 2016 SBS 2 2014, and One 2015 & 2016.

Question 184.
Q: How many players have won the MVP award three times each in the ANZ Championship, Trans-Tasman Netball League?
A: Two both Jamaican nationals, namely -
    Jhaniele Fowler-Reid (2013, 2015, 2016)
    Romelda Aiken (2015, 2008, 2009)

Question 185.
Q: How many different countries are represented in the Trans-Tasman Netball League MVPs?
A: Four, namely –
    Jamacia
    England
    Australia
    New Zealand

Question 186.
Q: How many players have won three ANZ Championship medals?
A: Six, namely –
      Laura Geitz
      Erin Bell
      Rebecca Bulley
      Caitlyn Nevis
      Romelda Aiken
      Clare McMeniman

Question 187.
Q: Who is the only player to have won three ANZ Championship medals with three different franchises?
A: Bec Bully – 2008 NSW Swifts, 2013 Adelaide Thunderbirds and 2015 QLD Firebirds.

Question 188.
Q: Who performed a rugby like Line-Out lift to defend the shot that infamously become known as the Harrison Hoist?
A: Anna Harrison and Kyla Cullen

COMMONWEALTH BANK TROPHY

Question 189.
Q: What year did the Commonwealth Bank Trophy start?
A: 1997

Question 190.
Q: Name the Commonwealth Bank Trophy teams that are now defunct?
A: AIS Canberra Darters
        Hunter Jaegers
        Sydney Swifts (Merged with Jaegers to NSW Swifts)
        Melbourne Kestrels
        Melbourne Pheonix
        Perth Orioles
        Adelaide Ravens
        Sydney Sandpipers

THE UTIMATE NETBALL TRIVIA BOOK

Question 191.
Q: How many years did the Commonwealth Bank Trophy last for?
A: 10 years – ending after the 2007 season.

Question 192.
Q: Who was the most successful team in the Commonwealth Bank Trophy?
A: The Melbourne Phoenix – winning 5 / 10 championships

Question 193.
Q: Which two teams played each other in every Commonwealth Bank Trophy grand final except one?
A: Sydney Swifts and the Melbourne Phoenix.

Question 194.
Q: How many founding teams were there in the Commonwealth Bank Trophy?
A: Eight

Question 195.
Q: What were the Commonwealth Bank Trophy teams named after?
A: Native Bird

Question 196.
Q: Which player was awarded MVP four times over the ten years, the most across the league?
A: Sharelle McMahon – 2000, 2003, 2006 & 2007

Question 197.
Q: Which two players have won Grand Final MVP twice in the Commonwealth Bank Trophy?
A: Sharelle McMahon (2002 & 2000) and
       Liz Ellis (2001 & 2006)

Question 198.
Q: Which coach women coach of the year 3 out of 4 times the award was given?
A: Julie Fitzgerald with the Sydney Swifts.

Question 199.
Q: Who was the broadcaster for the Commonwealth Bank Trophy?
A: ABC

NATIONAL BANK CUP

Question 200.
Q: What year did the inaugural National Bank Cup commence?
A: 1998

Question 201.
Q: How many years did the National Bank Cup run for?
A: 9 years – from 1998 to 2007.

Question 202.
Q: Before National Bank, what company was the naming sponsor of the league?
A: Coca Cola

Question 203.
Q: Who were the most successful team in the National Bank Cup winning 7 titles?
A: Southern Sting

Question 204.
Q: Who was the TV broadcast partner?
A: ONESport

Question 205.
Q: How many teams were in the National Bank Cup the inaugural season?
A: 10, namely –
    Auckland Diamonds
    Bay of Plenty Magic
    Capital Shakers
    Canterbury Flames
    Counties Manukau Cometz
    Northern Force
    Otago Rebels
    Southern Sting
    Waikato Wildcats
    Western Flyers

THE BUSINESS OF NETBALL

Question 206.
Q: What is the average pay for a Suncorp Super Netball player in 2023?
A: $86,500 AUD based on a salary cap of $692,000 AUD per team.

Question 207.
Q: Who was announced as the major sponsor of the Australian Diamonds committing $15m AUD?
A: Visit Victoria

Question 208.
Q: True or False – Netball was one of the Foundational member sports of Australian Institute of Sport (AIS) at its creation in1981?
A: True

Question 209.
Q: In the latest estimates from World Netball, how many people were estimated to play Netball worldwide?
A: Over 20 million worldwide.

Question 210.
Q: What is the average player pay in the ANZ Championship in 2023?
A: $63,333 NZD based on a salary cap of $380,000

Question 211.
Q: What is the average player pay in the Vitality Super league in 2023?
A: £38,000 based on a salary cap of £380,000 per team/

ABOUT THE AUTHOR

Nina Lee is an accomplished sports enthusiast, writer, and passionate advocate for women's athletics. With a lifelong love for sports, Nina Lee has dedicated their career to promoting and celebrating the world of sport. Their expertise in this fast-paced and exhilarating sport is evident in their latest creation, a trivia book that delves deep into the fascinating world of netball.

Nina Lee is a firm believer in the power of trivia to connect fans of all ages to their favorite sports. They understand that trivia not only entertains but also educates, fostering a deeper appreciation for the sport. In their trivia book, readers can expect to find a wide range of questions and facts, from the basic rules and terminology to obscure anecdotes and remarkable achievements in netball history.

Whether you're a dedicated player, a die-hard fan, or simply curious about this dynamic sport, Nina Lee's book promises to entertain, inform, and inspire a new generation of netball enthusiasts. Join them on a journey through the thrilling world of netball, one question at a time, and discover just how much you didn't know about this incredible sport.

Printed in Dunstable, United Kingdom